To the Edge

BROKEN BUT MADE WHOLE DURING THE JOURNEY

Regina Breeze

ISBN: 978-0-615-96926-8

Published by: Lolana Mack Publishing

Layout: Write On Promotions

Cover Design: Koacher Design and Technology

Table of Contents

Foreword

My mother is corny in her own way, fun, intelligent, beautiful, caring and loving, but Regina M. Breeze is one to mask her feelings and emotions when it is beneficial to others. She is one to never tell us what's really wrong, but because I am her daughter, I can always tell when something is 'not right' with her. I had no idea that she was broken. She kept that from my brother and me for a long time, but I finally found out once her book was written. I had no idea what she was doing. We just knew that she was at her desk everyday typing away at her keyboard. When she explained the book, her exact words were, "God has told me write a book, so I am going to do that because that is what God wants me to do." She was walking in her calling and fulfilling her purpose. The book is about the journey that my mother took to become whole...again. She was broken and went to God to help her pick up the pieces to put them together again. This book was written to inspire women and to teach a lesson that says that you should strive to get to the edge of life and when you get to the edge you should jump and then soar.

Maya Breeze

My mother, Regina Breeze, is a beautiful, highly exceptional, thoughtful, caring, smart woman. She is the special one that I can share my ideas with, and will push me relentlessly to get them out, and to achieve my goals. My mother does not know how special she is, how much I love her, or how much she does, only to get so little back. She buys things for people, she cares for them, she sacrifices a lot, even when she had nothing herself. When she lost her job, we downsized to a smaller place to save her and her two oblivious children from going broke. Because she is exceptional to me, I decided to do something to let her know how much I care about her, I sacrificed (as she does for me) asked to move to my dad and step-mother's home. I could tell my mother was heartbroken when I made the decision, but it was for 'our' good. Now just that and a thousand more reasons, I just wanted her to know how much I love her. She is my mother, she is my Queen, and no words can describe how much she is adored.

My Mother's new and first of many books, will be an amazing spiritual experience for women, men, and even children. It can and will lift you up where you might have been torn down. It will move and make you crave more that will come soon enough. For this little bit of my mom's creativeness I am sincerely proud of her! For this she will accomplish many of her goals and amaze many as always.

Calvin Breeze, Jr.

So begins the book of a life of losses and gains, bitter and sweet lessons of loving and learning to become whole. Have you taken the time to look at the reflections of your life? Try it and discover how different and the same you are with those seeking purpose. In the peace of the reflection you may find joy, contentment and private unshakeable experiences. However, in the noise you may find loneliness, bitterness and confusion. Regina once shared all of these spaces with you and through those experiences she found the courage to look beyond her personal self, her comfortable woes and her privacy to seek refuge. Refuge that would only come once she screamed for help. Courage allowed her to invite you to be consistence in her quest.

Regina is a woman who did not give herself permission to feel, hurt, cry or complain out loud. She buried her 'true self' deep in, what she felt like was a safe place. Her eye-opening discovery was that she was not safe, even inside her own heart. Her realization came from eloquent attempts to conceal her thoughts, passions and dreams which ultimately become transparent. Without doubt; those who were careful and paying close attention were not frightened by her new presence, instead overjoyed. You will enjoy reading how she stands still in her space, takes small steps to walk out of the fog and giant leaps into the light as she goes to the edge. Her compelling story is a testament of how strength and order will propel us into self-discovery.

Regina is an author who shares the transformation of her life with hopes of it benefitting those who read her book. The transformation did not come over night, nor through one or ten lessons, it was developed after she admittedly decided not to be broken. Imagine walking around for years and one day realizing the heel on your shoe is broken. You have two choices; you can repair it or focus on the damage you think you did for whatever length of time it was broken. Regina made a decision that she knew would not necessarily be easy. Repair it! This well-written detail-oriented novel (book/journal) can be used as an eye-opening approach to self-stepping stones of inspiration for women.

God named us human beings for a reason…to continue being. As Regina walked to the edge she found truth and the essence of knowing "no one has to suffer brokenness for others to be whole".

Linda Proctor Merritt

To the Edge

Broken but Made Whole During the Journey

The Beginning

We cannot abandon life because of its storms. The strongest trees are not found sheltered in the safety of the forest, rather they are in the open spaces – bent and twisted by winds of all seasons. God provides deep roots when there are wide – spreading branches.

- Tammy Felton

The story began where I thought my life was ending. My husband, Calvin and I moved to Atlanta, Georgia. We had been married for a little over nine years and had two wonderful children. Maya was four at the time and Calvin Jr. was one. I was devastated and could not understand why God was moving us to Atlanta. I was so close to my family and they could not understand it either. The only other time I had been away was when I went to College and that was right there in Clemson, South Carolina, only an hour or so away. I could drive home any day I wanted after class and drive back to school the next morning. I remember the day we began packing up and saying goodbye. Secretly, I was asking questions like: Why? How long we would have to stay? Who would be there to help out with the children? Just to name a few. My mother had watched Maya while we worked until she was old enough to start school. Calvin Jr. though was just a baby and I was terrified of putting him in daycare before he could talk and tell me what was going on. We would have to make new friends, find a new church to attend and basically start over in a new city. I had to tuck that scared little girl away and put on my brave face and assure my mother and sisters that everything was ok and that I was excited about the move. Calvin and his partner were going to start their own business and everything would be fine. In my brief alone moments, I would ask God why we had to move here and I would wait to hear confirmation. I heard nothing. I had no idea what was awaiting me in Atlanta, but if I had, I probably would have refused to move at that time. God was not giving me details, but deep down, I knew it was his will that we move.

> DON'T BE AFRAID
> TO GIVE UP THE
> GOOD TO GO FOR
> THE GREAT
>
> -KENNY ROGERS

Shortly after we arrived, on our 10 year anniversary, there was talk of a separation, or even worse, divorce. We had just begun to settle in good to our new life in Atlanta. This was absolutely absurd, I thought. My response was quite emphatic. "I don't know what the problem is but you had better get it together, I did not get married to be divorced and I did not have children to become single with children. So whatever you need to do to figure it out, you do that and get it together. Divorce is not an option!" After I made this statement, things continued to go downhill. Life as I knew it was no more and I experienced more hurt and pain than I ever thought I could possibly handle. This was why we had to move to Atlanta. God was beginning to shake up my cozy world; getting me out of my comfort zone. I realized that had I still been at home with my family, I would have them to lean on (as I always did) instead of God. It was time for me to grow up and follow and know God for myself. I was not ready for where God was calling me and he knew that. This did not change the fact that it was time and I could no longer avoid my journey with him. As this journey began, I suffered in silence. Never telling my family back home what was going on. I had always been a private person and I did not want to make them worry about me or for them to come to my rescue. Plus I knew that you should never involve your family in your marriage, especially when you are having issues. I could just hear them saying come home, and as much as I hated the way I was feeling and the fact that I had been relocated, deep down in my heart I knew that it was a move of God and that I was supposed to be here. I was being stretched. Stretched beyond what I ever thought possible.

As I sat on my king-sized bed looking around the room filled with clutter, I wondered how this happened and how I should fix it. The room seemed to mirror my mind at the time, with its disheveled appearance. Every space was filled with something that should not be there. I had always been very neat and conscientious. Clean clothes were on the chair, dirty clothes were in the basket, what was known as my desk was now covered with books and stacks of out of order paper. At that exact moment I felt extremely overwhelmed. Simultaneously I had several thoughts dancing in my head. Where do I go from here? How do I fix my life? How can I earn extra money? How can I pay this bill, that bill and those bills? How do I make this dream and that dream come true, are my children ok and will they be able to handle all of the changes? It was all too much for me today as tears started to form in my eyes. My head was hurting and my stomach was rumbling. I had felt bad for the past few days with symptoms that included a bad headache, nausea, vomiting and diarrhea. Perhaps my body was feeling the effects of my scattered, overwhelmed mind and my clutter-filled room.

I have heard all of my life that prayer works and that prayer changes things. I was at a point in my life where I needed to see that on a major scale. No more of the miracles I heard or read in the Bible, I needed to see miracles manifested in my very own life. I knew what the bible said, I was what many called a church baby. Born and reared in a pious environment, attending Church on Sunday and at least two other days a week. I read and memorized scriptures as a child. Every Christmas and Easter service, there I was reciting this passage or that passage and singing this song or that song I had to learn. In some ways, I think growing up in this manner made it a little harder to get to know God for myself. I was sincere about my walk, but I did not always trust him as I should. Here I was away from my family and it gave new meaning to the scripture, "God will never leave us nor forsake us." No matter how alone I felt, I was not alone. It is easier to quote a scripture than it is to stand on it. There finally came a time in my life where I could not just talk Faith but I had to stand on it and walk life out by faith.

> YOUR ACTIONS SPEAK
> SO LOUD, I CANNOT
> HEAR WHAT YOU ARE
> SAYING.
>
> -RALPH WALDO
> EMERSON

One of the first scriptures I learned was Hebrews 11:1, "Now Faith is the substance of things hoped for and the evidence of things not seen." Our actions speak louder than words. My actions began to scream that I was weak in my faith. I was guilty of walking by sight, not by faith and fearing what I couldn't see. I had to begin to build my faith and make a conscious decision to live by faith every day. I heard a minister say once that as believers, we have the right to look beyond our now into our future and command our future for our now. That reminds me of calling those things that be not as though they were (Romans 4:17). Just like our words have power, our faith is powerful when put to action.

As I sat on my bed with these thoughts in my head, I cried out to God, in the midst of my tears, I heard him plainly say, "If you take care of my business, I will take care of yours." I stopped in mid tear and listened for more. No more was said to me at that moment. Those words were profound and I often think back on that day and feel encouraged. I asked God over and over, "What do you want me to do?" I heard nothing more. But in the midst of living and living for God, I was begging to hear more.

I heard T.D. Jakes one day say that God will give me strength to love him if he stays and strength to live without him if he leaves. God did just that for me and more. My husband and I had been together since I was a freshman in college and married the day after graduation. I could not imagine life without him, being divorced, and much less being single with children. I had no fear of being a single mother because he had always been a wonderful father and I knew that would not change.

The harder I tried to hold on, the worse things got. One day, I was out popping firecrackers with a friend and I was not familiar with this type of firecracker so he gave me specific instructions. Light the end and don't hold the firecracker too tight but don't throw it either. It is a matter of holding it gently and releasing it at the right time, once it is lit. He showed me how to do it and when it was my turn, I held the firecracker too tight for too long and it almost hurt both of us. This was funny after we realized no one was hurt. This incident reminded me of a time when I was six years old. I was out with some cousins popping firecrackers and I let the firecracker explode in my hand because I continued to hold it when I should have let it go. There was a valuable lesson for me in the firecrackers. I did not follow the instructions. If you hold something too long (when it wants or needs to be released) it will end up hurting you. It's all in the timing. Don't hold on to it too tight, don't throw it away too quickly either, just loosen your grip and gently release it. People have said, "If you hold your hand closed tightly, nothing can go out and nothing can come in." Apparently God had specific plans for me and at that point in my life I could not bear to think of what that could be because all I could focus on was what I thought I was losing. I kept asking God, why he brought me all the way to Atlanta, away from what I knew and allowed my family to fall apart?

While suffering silently, I was forced to be there for others. One day while at work a co-worker came in and just dropped to her knees and put her head in my lap and started bawling. She told me how she and her husband were struggling in their marriage and she did not know what to do. She asked me to pray for her. I felt awful and felt that I could not pray or encourage her because of my own situation. After praying, I realized that I was exactly the one to help her. Often God will use us in an area to help someone else when we are hurting or in need in that very same area. If you were abused as a child, then you understand what it feels like and can help a child dealing with abuse. Or help a parent understand what his or her child may be feeling after being abused. If you have been divorced, rejected, sick, raped, homeless, suffered from low or no self-esteem, you have compassion to help others in the same or similar situation. More often than not we must help others before we are healed from our own issues.

Sometimes we are even healed ourselves by helping others.

"For I reckon that the sufferings of this present time are not worthy to be compared with the glory which shall be revealed in us." Romans 8:18

God was calling me and I was not listening.

Not Broken Enough

"It is doubtful whether God can bless a man greatly until he has hurt him deeply"
- A.W. Tozer

Shortly after things became really rough at home, Tiffany, one of my old friends from college and I decided to meet up in Florida for a Mother's Day trip. On Sunday morning, we went to church, the service was wonderful. Afterwards, we stood in a long line to purchase some CD's from the media department. A woman named Pam, that was working the line, came over to assist me. She kept looking at me and she finally said, "wait right here." When she returned, she had several CD's in her hand and she said, "Here, I want you to listen to these." The CDs were dealing with love and marriage. I was puzzled, but I took them and said, "Thank You." She then started talking to me as if she knew me and my situation, telling me things that only God knew in a very short period of time. Pam was a very "in your face" person with a very dominant personality and this was quite offensive to me initially. She began to tell me how I was not yet humble and how I was not broken enough. This was funny to me because I was feeling just the opposite. All the hurt, pain, and loneliness that I was feeling and I was not humble or broken enough!? I was getting angry because my heart felt like it was broken. She was mistaken and what did she know anyway? She did not know me! She told me a little about her own situation and some things that she had gone through in her own marriage. These thoughts and feelings I was having, show that no matter how much we love God and try to do right, we can still be (and often are) in denial about our issues and our situations.

> THE TIME THAT I
> AM IN IS THE
> ONLY TIME I
> KNOW I HAVE
>
> -LPROCTORM

Pam asked Tiffany and me to meet her for breakfast the next morning so that we could talk more before we left Florida. I had heard enough, but I reluctantly agreed. I was very respectful and listened to all that she said with an open heart for God. She was clearly telling me the truth but I was just not ready or able to receive it. I guess I was blinded by my own hurt. Thought it was funny that God used a total stranger, someone in a totally different state to speak to me on this level. Finally I decided to open up to Pam. God knows what we need, when we need it, because I would not have opened up and spoken about it to anyone else at that time. Never once did I ever consider asking God to break me in order to make me. I had just begun asking him to change me after years of asking him to change my husband and to change my situation. Who would have ever thought that years later, I would realize that I was broken.

I did not just wake up one morning changed. God took me through many ups and downs, painful situations, turned up the heat, and broke me in order to change me and make me over. I heard someone say once, that "When God wants to do an impossible task; he takes an impossible person and crushes him." Now when I say I am humble, I know without any doubt that I am humble. Through life's experiences, pain, sorrow, hurt, and God's refining and polishing me, I am humble. Little did I know, this was only the beginning.

WHEN CIRCUMSTANCES SEEM IMPOSSIBLE, WHEN ALL SIGNS OF GRACE IN YOU SEEM AT THEIR LOWEST EBB, WHEN THE TEMPTATION IS FIERCEST, WHEN LOVE AND JOY AND HOPE SEEM WELL NIGH EXTINGUISHED IN YOUR HEART, THEN REST, WITHOUT FEELING AND WITHOUT EMOTION, IN THE FATHER'S FAITHFULNESS.

D. TRYON

On the days that I was hurting the most, I would go to work with a smile and say that everything was great. One of the people, God used in my life to make a change was a guy that I had worked with for years named Johnny. He would always see past the smile and know when I was masking the pain. He would immediately start to tell me about his Pastor's message from church on the previous Sunday or what he heard T.D. Jakes say. The more I tried to avoid him, the more I had to deal with him. Finally, one day I went to work and found that Johnny was my new director. Working more closely together, he began to speak powerful words of encouragement into my life. He started to say that I was a sleeping giant and I needed to wake up and stop acting like a Twinkie. He was relentless and did not care that I did not want to hear it. Every day Johnny would say that I needed to wake up and stop being a sleeping giant. I never told him but I began to break down the words and really see how they applied to me. Sleeping is the condition of being asleep. A giant is a person or thing of unusually great size, power, importance, etc...; greater or more eminent than others. A Twinkie is a small sponge cake with a synthetic cream filling. It is very sweet and good. However, it is extremely delicate, easily mashed, must be handled gently and is not easy to travel with. If I am viewed as a person with great power, worth and importance but am acting like someone that is too soft, weak and must be handled with care, I must not know my worth or my full potential. I must not have known who I was. "I am a child of the King" and "God Favors Me". I was highly offended by Johnny calling me a Twinkie. His job was done. He made me realize some things about myself and how I needed to step up to the plate and be what God has called me to be. The bible tells us in Luke 12:48 that to whom much is given much is required: and to whom men have committed much, of him they will ask the more. I began to consider my actions, my plans, my goals and ask God what I needed to change about myself in order to be what he had created me to be.

I was listening to T.D. Jakes one day and he said that we should stop running from how God created us, and that we are more useful free than we are running. Immediately, I was reminded of something that I had read, written by Marianne Williamson, which says, "Our deepest fear is not that we are inadequate. Our deepest fear is that we are powerful beyond measure. It is our light, not our darkness that most frightens us. We ask ourselves, who am I to be brilliant, gorgeous, talented, fabulous? Actually, who are you not to be? You are a child of God. You playing small does not serve the world. There is nothing enlightened about shrinking so that other people won't feel insecure around you. We are all meant to shine, as children do. We were born to make manifest the glory of God that is within us. It's not just in some of us; it's in everyone. And as we let our own light shine, we unconsciously give other people permission to do the same. As we are liberated from our own fear, our presence automatically liberates others."

One thing that my husband always told me was that I was not living up to my fullest potential. He would continue and say that I was not allowing myself to be the person that God had called me to be. It is true that I was always comfortable helping others by pushing them to be successful. I was the Assistant who made the Executive look good, I was the Speech Writer that made the Speaker sound great, I was the one who prepared the presentation that made the presenter look good. God wanted me out of that comfort zone and I was fighting to stay there. The pain that I was feeling was not just about the possibility of losing my marriage; God was forcing me to deal with me and face the fact that I was not being all that he had called me to be. I decided to strive to seek God to be the person I was created to be and I would no longer make excuses for not being who I should be. God has the blueprint for all of our lives and he knows just who he created us to be. . He would not put any more on me than I could bear which made it evident that I could handle all that I was going through.

God was calling me and I was not listening.

The Transformation

Am I My Brother's Keeper?

"Bond through success and failure"
-LProctorM

Everyone has that defining moment with God. Some have it early in life while others have it much later in life. There's a moment where we actually 'get it' and things begin to click for us. I happened to have my defining moments, life changing events and surrendering myself completely to God later in life. I breezed through my childhood, teenage years and college years. Making good grades, doing well in sports and music, having my family around me, and things seemed naturally easy. I was vivacious and care free. Having it easy does not challenge one's faith. I am sure that God had been doing little subtle things in me as he does in all of us. However, it just seemed like suddenly, one day I looked back and saw that the changes had been taking place all along.

One day as I sat talking with my friend Linda Proctor-Merritt, she told me about a conversation that she had with a male friend of hers. He asked her to tell him something important about herself and she said "I am not broken". As she said the words, "I am not broken", immediately my eyes began to well up with tears and no matter how hard I tried not to blink out of fear that tears would fall, they began to stream down my face and lap under my chin. It was at that very moment (with much chagrin) that I realized that I was BROKEN. It instantly felt as if a ton of bricks had fallen quietly and hit me over the head and then the red lights began flashing along with the loud siren ringing as if there was an emergency. The problem was that no one felt the bricks or saw the flashing lights or heard the siren ringing but me. I did not explain to Linda just how great of an impact her words had on me at that very moment because I was too emotional. This really took me some place else. God had this moment and conversation at the appointed time for me to realize one of the most important things about myself and he used Linda to do it. She was very instrumental in my journey from this point on. I would tell her things that were bothering me and her outlook was so incredibly different from mine that I would wonder, "Are we talking about the same situation?" God has blessed her with the gift of bringing a sense of clarity to things that seem so confusing and unclear to others, without even giving it much thought.

So what does broken mean? The definition is to be ruptured, torn, fractured, or fragmented; Not functioning properly or out of working order. For a long time, I had not been functioning properly. I began that day, to understand I had a serious problem and only God could help me. My new daily prayer was that God would make me whole. It felt so awful to be grown and married with children and have to admit that I was broken and had been for a very long time. However, in a strange way, it felt so much better to finally be able to say exactly what the problem was. I was broken; not crazy, not depressed, not alone, not incapable of being happy or joyful, just plain broken (which was causing all of the aforementioned feelings). See my husband knew this even before I did. I just don't believe that he knew himself how to verbalize it to me. Moving to Atlanta, away from both of our families and what we had grown accustomed to, we just knew that we could have a fresh start and be happier, but it really exposed me even more. I could not explain it because I could not even understand it. Had the ideal situation; a great husband, two beautiful children, a degree and a job, yet I still was not happy. The fact of the matter was that no matter where I was, who I was with, what I had or what I was doing, as long as I was broken, I would remain the same. Calvin just kept saying that I was not happy but he did not know how to make me happy and it was painful for him. When in all actuality, I was broken and he did not know how to fix me because only God could do that. My husband and my children were the glue that was keeping me stuck together in spite of all of my brokenness. I made them my everything. I did not spend time with any friends and did not let anyone into my circle and would not allow myself to have a life outside of my family. This was not good and it was not healthy. I realize now that I was holding on for dear life because away from them I would have to deal with me and I did not know how to do that anymore. They knew that I was not happy and that something was wrong but they did not know what to do. I did not know how to function outside of them, so it was easier to stick with the glue. It was so much easier to take care of their every need than it was to take care of me. Being there for them was the only thing that remotely made me feel alive. My family was what made me feel normal, my everything. Outside of my family, the only other thing that helped me was staying busy. When we resist what God wants us to do, we have to find ways to avoid it. In order to be accountable for my time, I would continue to find important things to do to stay busy and while I was doing them, I felt better. In reality, I was not being fulfilled; rather it was making me feel even emptier. Every time I completed one project, I would quickly move on to the next. I took great pride in these accomplishments and would put my all into them. Looking back at my life, I see where I was not fulfilled. I completed my Associates, then my Bachelors, then went back for some Accounting courses Since that was not enough,

I took bookkeeping classes, passed the state board exam and earned a Real Estate license, After that I went back for DHR Training certification. When things got really tough for me, I went back to school and earned an MBA. While completing my MBA, I was going through my divorce and only one or two people knew it. I was working a full time job, going to school, working as the church administrator in the church that I was attending, and taking care of my family. The more stress I felt, the more work I would put on myself. I was determined to make an A in every class and I successfully did that. As I completed one thing, I quickly asked, "Ok what is next?" Then as I started to enroll for a Doctorate, I said, "Regina, why don't you stop and learn more about God?" So instead I began taking some Bible classes. I began to hunger and thirst to know more about God. The more I sought him, the more he worked in me. My pastors, Apostle Keith and Prophetess Shalita Wyett were very instrumental in this part of my transformation. They were always encouraging, always instructing, and always pushing.

God began using people in my life as solvent to loosen the glue that was holding me together.

I had lived a sheltered and very guarded childhood. As I grew up I was always afraid that trusting people would result in my being hurt. So I learned very early to guard myself. There was a wall around me that was not easily penetrated. I did not have many friends that I talked to about anything important. I have always been a great friend to others, but would never allow them to be a real friend to me. Friendship goes both ways, and people that truly care don't like to be shut out and they want to reciprocate the friendship. Because of this, I learned to suppress and internalize my true feelings. No matter what happened or what I really felt, I was ok. My husband broke this barrier and I put all of my trust in him. When he showed me he was human, it became harder for me to let others in. I believe this was the beginning of God showing me that I should not put my trust in man but in him only. He is a jealous God and showed me that although my husband loved me, he was not perfect. After my divorce, part of the glue that was holding my broken pieces was stripped away. When the children started having to spend time with their father and away from me, even more of the glue was stripped away. This was really painful and I really resisted having them away from me so much. Most women have the complaint that their children's father won't spend any time with the children. My complaint was that he wanted to spend so much time with them that I was forced to share them which meant I would then have to spend a lot of time alone. I slowly began to open up and allow myself to trust a few people. This was God working on me and I went from talking to no one to having many people that he strategically placed in my life that I could talk to and draw from at any given point. Little did I know he would use certain people as solvent to help strip away the balance of the glue that had held me together for so long. It would be replaced with God's power and anointing which makes us whole. Throughout the transition there were at least seven people that came into my life. They have all been a huge blessing in one way or another. They are all special to me and have all contributed to my journey from broken, to stripped, to transformed, and ultimately to new. I was always reminded to enjoy the journey. It is so easy to get hung up on the fact that we are not where we want to be and that we don't like the feeling of being just where we are that we don't take the time to enjoy the journey. If we were traveling across the country from East Coast to the West Coast in a car, it would be a shame to be so disappointed in the fact that we had to drive instead of fly that we didn't take the time to enjoy the beautiful scenery as we were driving. We must learn all that we can from each experience during our journey and make the best of it. The journey is what makes getting to the destination so much more fun.

I think each person in my life held a piece of the puzzle to my life. Two out of the seven of them have seemed more like a gift from God. We could discuss everything under the sun and I knew it would never be repeated nor did I feel I was being judged. Everyone needs someone to hold them accountable. These people would listen to me and would pray for me, when it seemed that everyone else around me wanted me to pray and give to them.

For many years, I had pondered the scripture (Nehemiah 8:10) "The Joy of the Lord is my strength". I questioned why I never felt joyous. Does this mean I have no strength? Am I weak? If I have no joy and the joy of the Lord is my strength then by deductive reasoning, I must be weak. I began asking God for joy, everlasting joy. As I grew in grace and sought God more, I realized that much like happiness, having joy is also a choice. If you believe in God and love him, you must choose to find the joy in serving him. The more you seek to please him, the more joy you will have. No matter what is going on around you, you should feel the joy of the Lord on the inside. Whenever things were really hard, Linda Proctor-Merritt would always say that I have to choose to go through the situation with joy instead of pain.

Twelve, thirteen, fourteen, fifteen; finally I dropped the bar down on the rack. "Good job", everyone cheered. I am determined to exercise my body the same way I have been exercising my spirit through fasting, worshipping and praying. I am finally finding my way. Every time I finish a set,

Joshua adds more weight to the bar. When I say, "No", he says, "Yes, you can handle it Regina, let's go!" This is a sign of a good trainer. They learn how to deal with their trainees and they know how to motivate them to do more than they think they can do. As I do my reps, if I stop and rack the bar before finishing my set, he will tack on at least two more. I didn't like it at the time, but I do appreciate the challenge and the accountability that he gives me. If I try to stop, he says, "oh ok you're only cheating yourself."

When we are going through with God, he knows each of us and he knows how much we can bear. We don't have a choice in the test. God chooses how to test us and just how much pressure to apply. If we stop before completing the test, God will have us start over at the beginning and keep retaking the test until we pass it.

I am reminded of how coins are made.... Heat is applied again and again and the silver is cleaned and polished. Sliver goes into a casting furnace at 2100 degrees Fahrenheit. Here the silver is melted into a continuous bar. From here the bar goes through the roughing mill, which consists of two rollers that squash the bar in order to flatten. It uses up to nine tons of force and this process is repeated a dozen times to flatten the bar to the desired size. The finishing mill thins the strip out even more to get to the size that the coin should be for its intended use. The blanking machine cuts out blanks. Because the metal can become brittle and crack and break when struck, it goes through an annihilating furnace repeatedly. Under a high concentrated amount of pressure, each coin is made one at a time and heavy pressure is applied to hold it in place. One of the final steps is having the engraver add the design and stamp the date on the coins. If the coin is moved or gets out of place during any step of the process, it must be scrapped and must go through the process again from the beginning. The result is a shiny, beautiful coin.

In this walk, after going through so much heat and pressure going in and out of the furnace of life, I would not want to get out of place and have to start the process all over again. The pressure does not feel good at all and at times it is nearly unbearable, but the thing to remember is that I am being polished and finished which also means being authenticated and validated. Once I get through the process, God will stamp his seal of approval on me and the result will be a polished, refined, transformed, whole, new Regina. I will then be a woman that God can trust and that he can use.

-God was calling me and I was not listening.

Out of the Mouth of a Child

"It is easier to build strong children than to repair broken men."
-Fredrick Douglass

My son began showing signs of depression, and quickly after much prayer and discussing we sought out a therapist for him to talk to. Finally an appointment was made and the four of us went to see the therapist. She asked to see me after first speaking with Little Calvin. She asked me how I was handling the divorce and how I was dealing with all of the added stress. Like always, I declared, "Oh, I am fine, everything is well with me, we just need to make sure my son is ok, that's why we are here." "I understand," she said as if she was going along with my story, "Well that is funny because your son says that you are not ok." She said that he is hurting and getting depressed because he is worried about me. He told her that I pretend I am ok but I am not and that he just wants me to be happy. As I sat in the chair, my body went numb and the tears were welling up inside of me. Anger and sadness struck me and I began to get a little defensive. "So this is my fault?" I thought to myself. The last thing I ever wanted to do was cause my children any pain. I prayed and cried all night long and when I awoke the next morning, the facts were still there and I had to face what had been said about me the previous night. Could he be right? Was I pretending to be ok? I must have been doing a terrible job, though my son was always good at discerning the truth.

After the next session with the therapist, the consensus was that I was the problem. My brokenness and unhappiness had caused my husband to be unhappy and was now causing my children to be unhappy as well. Secretly, I asked God, "Will I ever be happy? Will I ever have joy?" As we left the office, there seemed to be a huge elephant walking with us. The elephant got into the car with us and was sucking up all of the oxygen in the car. Naturally it felt that there was not enough room and I felt really small. I could hardly breathe. We rode home in silence. No radio, no talking, it felt as though we were all even afraid to make any sudden moves. Calvin Sr. dropped the kids and me off and he went home. As soon as we walked in the door, I went straight to my room. None of the usual instructions were given. No get your clothes out for school tomorrow, be sure your homework is finished and your backpacks packed, no take your baths and get ready for bed, no take the dog out, nothing. I mustered up enough strength to peel my clothes off, and change without even taking my normal shower before bed. I crawled in the bed feeling numb and lifeless. After covering my head completely with the covers, there was no energy to cry, speak, feel angry, or to even pray. I just wanted to go to sleep with the hope of waking up and realizing this was all a dream. Well it was not a dream, though it felt like a nightmare and the issue was still very much so present when I woke but at least now I was able to pray. My heart was really overwhelmed. The feeling of depression was overwhelmingly strong. How could I

> LOVE IS LOVE IS A POWERFUL EMOTION THAT IS SHARED BETWEEN TWO PEOPLE THAT ARE IMPORTANT TO EACH OTHER.
>
> MAYA - 14

be causing the three people that I love the most in my life to be so unhappy, when I was trying so hard to keep my unhappiness from them? There is definitely truth to the saying that if mom is not happy then no one is happy in the home. All at the same time there was a "Yes" in my spirit. All I wanted to say to God was yes. Just keep digging in me and remove all that is not like you. Do whatever you need to do to change me and make me whole. I was so sincere about this because I was at a point in my life where I knew I needed to change and I wanted to. That's how it has to be. No matter what you go through in life, there comes a time when you have to say, "Lord, change me! No matter what you have to do, just change me!"

There was another instance where God used my son to show me myself. They had just come home from a week with their father and it happened to be Mother's Day. He kept looking at me and then he said that he wanted to call daddy back because he wanted us to have a family meeting. He called the family meeting and basically said, "Look, we need to make some changes in this family." He did not like all of the tension and frustration. He cried and passionately articulated himself very well. He pointed out to me what I was doing that he did not like and I was so overwhelmed with how proud of him I was for speaking up so eloquently. All I could say was, "Happy Mother's Day to me!" I was thanking God for giving us such wonderful children and especially this son for being so straight-forward and attentive and for caring enough to call even me on my behavior. From that day on, I have been conscious of the fact that he knows much more than I give him credit for and I cannot pretend in his presence.

Yet another instance, we were all out in a public place and my husband had moved on and was in a relationship with someone else. This was still new for me and I had never seen him show affection toward another woman. As he put his arm around his girlfriend, I was oblivious to the fact that I showed any emotion or expression at all until I felt a tap on my shoulder. I quickly looked over at my son as he shook his head, "No". I said "what?" He said mommy, don't do that to yourself and I then made a futile attempt to evade by saying, "What are you talking about?" He said more emphatically this time,

LOVE IS THE REASON THAT WE ARE HERE. WITHOUT LOVE, GOD WOULD NOT HAVE MADE US AND HE WOULD NOT HAVE BEEN SO TOLERANT WITH US OVER THE YEARS THAT WE HAVE MADE SO MANY MISTAKES.

Calvin - 11

"I watched you watch them and I don't want you to do that to yourself, you don't care about that at all!" I finally said, "Thank you, son. You are absolutely right, I don't care and I am fine." This again made me feel so proud that at eleven years old, my son was looking out for me in this manner. I felt that although he was our son, God had given him to me long ago for a reason. He was sent to watch over me. I thank God because he sacrificed his son to give me mine. He knew that the day would come that he would be the young man in my life encouraging me to keep it moving. He is always there to keep me on my toes. Both of my children are special, but my son just seems to tap into my emotions and my spirit in such an unusual way. When I was feeling the lowest in my brokenness, prior to and immediately following the divorce, my children were the reason that I got out of bed in the mornings. As parents, we invested so much time, effort and money into our children in hopes of giving them a great start in life. We sacrificed early on to have the money to send them to private schools, to pay for extracurricular activities, sports, music and so on. We had them in Church and taught them about God. We tried to teach them to be independent, strong and self-confident. Little Calvin always spoke his mind, and we did not want to break his spirit but we did want to curb it. It should not be a surprise that he uses what he has been taught to help me along my journey. He constantly gives back to me all that I tried to instill in him early on and reminds me of those small lessons and bits of wisdom. God has given him so much wisdom at such a young age. My daughter is attentive but is quiet with it, while my son is very vocal with it. It is important to remember that no matter how bad the pain is; life will go on with the help of God. We should also remember that God can use anyone (even our own children) to help us when we need it.

To the Edge

As parents, we must learn to listen to our children and hear what they say as well as what they don't say. We must pay attention to the way that they look and read what they are showing even with their mannerisms. We can learn a lot from them about life. They are often a reflection of us and can show us a lot about ourselves. God has charged us to "Train up a child in the way he should go. And when he is old he will not depart from it. " -Proverbs 22:6

We are responsible for fostering healthy environments for them and building strong children so that they grow into strong adults. Children are just little people that watch our every move and often mimic our actions. They look to see how you handle difficult situations and how you treat others, and often they can prepare others for how you may handle different situations. For this reason, it is very important to live an upright life in front of them and let them know that life is full of ups and downs. I had to learn that it is ok for them to know when I am hurting. It teaches them the reality of life. The lesson is not that life is perfect but in how we handle adversity. My children showed me that they knew much more than I gave them credit for and my not being honest about my pain was causing them pain. There were days that I woke up with my feelings exposed. I was hurting so bad that it felt like anyone who looked at me could see that my feelings had been transferred from the inside and were now being worn on the outside like my clothes. That was a miserable feeling because I knew that I had to hold it together. One wrong move could cause me to burst into tears and not stop crying. I would give the children all that I had throughout the day and rush them to bed at night and then cry myself to sleep. I can remember waking up a few mornings to them asking me what was wrong because my eyes were so puffy from crying. My daughter would just ask if I was ok, and my son would always ask if I was crying. The hardest part was not allowing them to see me break down and I thought I was protecting them.

They need to know that they are discerning correctly when they feel that something isn't right. If I continue to say that everything is ok when it is clearly not, they won't learn to trust their discerning abilities as they grow up and get involved in their own relationships and deal with their children and families. The important thing is not always what happens to you, but rather how you handle or respond to what happens to you. Think about it, would you want your child to act just like you? If you have children, are you proud of how they are being reared? Are you equipping them for life to the best of your ability? What you instill in them now is what will come out of them later. God has given them to us for a short period of time and we must make each moment count.

Whenever I felt that I was all by myself, I was reminded that I am never alone. In spite of any and all uncertainty God is there. Although it is hard to see God in the midst of a storm, we must trust that he is there.

– God was calling me and I was not listening.

The Teacher Must Learn the Lesson First

God's promise to the pure of heart is of that knowledge of himself through love which is eternal life: and the heart will be pure when it is filled with the love of God in all things and above all things. To be filled with such love is to have obtained the promises which exceed all that we can desire. –
John Burnaby

I had known for some time that there was a calling on my life and it was to teach God's word. I was not completely walking in it because I did not want all of the responsibility that comes along with it. The word plainly says in Timothy "Study to show thyself approved". It had been confirmed by several ministers that I respect and they were starting to press me to teach. My pastor at the time asked me to speak on one Sunday morning and I was terrified. I kept saying, "Lord, are you sure? Do you want me to do this?" I began to ask him what I should teach on. For a whole week, he gave me nothing so I was starting to research and plan my own lesson. Finally, one night while in bed, I was on the verge of sleep and heard a voice plainly say, "Guard your heart with all diligence, for out of it flows the issues of life." Immediately I knew that I was supposed to teach on the heart. My question for the lesson was, "What is the condition of your heart?"

In the natural, the human heart is the engine of human life. Beating almost 100,000 times a day, it is an organ that provides a continuous blood circulation through the cardiac cycle and is one of the most vital organs in the human body.

Without a beating heart there is no life. When a person experiences cardiac arrest, they can occasionally be revived but when the heartbeat cannot be restored, life is over. Many have a heart murmur and…So it is in the natural, so it is in the spiritual. In the spirit, if your heart is damaged and not beating properly, you can spiritually die.

People use several expressions regarding the heart and they show how important the heart is, but do we really understand how serious it is? For example, common expressions that we use are, "Bless your Heart" and "What is your heart telling you about this situation?" When someone wants to talk about something serious, they may say, "Let's get to the heart of the matter" and when someone puts their all into something, we say they do it whole heartedly.

What does God say about the heart? The word heart is mentioned 743 times in the bible and is used in various contexts.

The heart often represents a person's will, and it reveals a person's true nature and motivation. As my pastor always says, God wants our heart and not just our lips. You might be saying, "What does that mean?" Your spiritual state is changed when you give your heart to God. Knowing about God or speaking about God does not bring you into right

> **YOU CAN'T GIVE AWAY WHAT YOU DON'T HAVE**

relationship with him. Giving him your heart (the core of your being) is what makes the difference. Without a trusting heart, there is no salvation. God knows what is really in our heart, and he searches and tests the heart of man. He delights in those whose hearts truly belong to him. God even knows what is in our hearts and minds whether we speak it or not.

According to Jeremiah 17:10, "I the Lord search the hearts; I try the reigns, even to give every man according to his ways, and according to the fruit of his doings." In other words, God searches our heart and examines our mind and rewards us for what our conduct deserves.

Luke 21: 1-4 says, "And he looked up, and saw the rich men casting their gifts into the treasury.

And he saw also a certain poor widow casting in thither two mites. And he said, "Of a truth I say unto you, that this poor widow hath cast in more than they all: For all these have of their abundance cast in unto the offerings of God: but she of her penury hath cast in all the living that she had."

Here as Jesus observes the widow's offering, the significance of the action is driven by the heart. Jesus said that the widow gave more to the temple by giving 2 coins than those who put much more in because of what was in her heart. She gave all that she had.

In my search I found that there are evil thoughts of the heart and there are righteous thoughts of the heart.

Jeremiah 17:9 says "the heart is deceitful above all things and beyond cure." For this reason, we should not trust what our heart tells us at all times. God holds us accountable for listening to the deceitful messages that our heart tells us. Satan places temptation in the mind of men, but we do have an opportunity to reject that temptation.

John 13:1 -4 says, "Now before the feast of the Passover, when Jesus knew that his hour was come that he should depart out of this world unto the Father, having loved his own which were in the world, he loved them unto the end. And supper being ended, the devil having now put into the heart of Judas Iscariot, Simon's son, to betray him; Jesus knowing that the Father had given all things into his hands, and that he was come from God, and went to God. He riseth from supper, and laid aside his garments: and took a towel, and girded himself."

Here Satan puts it in the heart of Judas to betray Jesus. Judas does not resist the temptation but he falls for it.

Proverbs 4:23 says "Guard thy heart with all diligence; for out of it flows the issues of life.

As Christians we should always ask God for a new heart, a clean heart. When we have shortcomings in our lives, we must seek God to transform our minds because if not we will continue to act out of our old, unclean heart. If you have issues in your heart, whether they are outward issues that can be seen by man or issues that no one can see, we cannot pass them off by saying,

"This is just the way I am."

"God understands me."

"God knows my heart."

To the Edge

Yes God knows our heart but he is still expecting us to do right and he is holding us accountable.

Going through this lesson already provoked me to cry out to God and ask him to search my heart and remove anything that is not pleasing to him and give me a clean heart that I might serve him.

As for the righteous thoughts of the heart:

Psalm 37:4 says "Delight yourself also in the Lord and He shall give you the desires of your heart."

In order to remove the temptations of the flesh from the heart, we must present a willing heart to God; letting him perform whatever surgery is necessary. We must keep our heart with all diligence; for out of it are the issues of life.

The Heart is the Seat of Emotions.

What is in your heart can be seen in your emotions.

1) When you are afraid or faint hearted, the remedy is a courageous heart... Psalm 27:3 says, "Though a host should encamp against me, my heart shall not fear; though war should rise against me, in this will I be confident.

2)	When you are discouraged or losing heart, your heart can be strengthened... Psalm 27:13 says, "I had fainted, unless I had believed to see the goodness of the Lord in the land of the living."

When you are sad or in need of comfort, the grieving or sad heart can be refreshed or renewed. Ezekiel

> GUARD YOUR HEART WITH ALL DILIGENCE FOR OUT OF IT FLOWS THE ISSUES OF LIFE.

36:26 says, " A new heart also will I give you, and a new spirit will I put within you; and I will take away the stony heart out of your flesh and I will give you an heart of flesh.

3)	When you are broken hearted, Psalm 147:3 says, "He heals the broken hearted, and binds up their wounds."

My two favorite scriptures regarding the subject are "He heals my broken heart and binds up my wounds curing my pains and sorrows." Psalm 147:3 and "Guard your heart with all diligence for out of it flows the issues of life." Again, the heart is the core of our being and is the engine of human life. In the natural we know how vitally important the heart is, but do we understand the same in the spiritual realm?

I have learned that I have a high threshold for pain, physical pain that is. But emotionally, I will do whatever possible to avoid pain. I have had to learn that pain is a part of life and cannot be avoided. We cannot avoid living passionately in order to avoid being hurt. I have often heard that pain is weakness leaving and we cannot receive healing without pain. Guarding your heart does not mean just shutting people out or putting up a wall so that no one can get close to you. There must be a lot of effort put forth in order to effectively guard your heart. To guard means to watch over or shield from danger or harm; to keep watch. Diligence means constant and earnest effort to accomplish what is undertaken; persistent exertion of body or mind; *Law*. The degree of care and caution required by the circumstances of a person; *Obsolete* care; caution. We must guard what goes in as well as what comes out.

We all need to take the time to make a conscious effort to allow God to deal with our hearts.

I also began to ask God to show me the hearts of those around me. I wanted to know the true heart of the people I was dealing with.

There are some things buried deep in some of our hearts that are keeping us from giving it to God completely. Some have gotten their hearts broken in relationships and instead of allowing God to fix it or give us a new heart, we just move on to another relationship looking for comfort. Instead of allowing God to deal with matters of our heart, (sin, jealousy, malice, fear among others), we just declare that God knows our heart and he is forgiving.

> HE HEALS MY BROKEN HEART AND BINDS UP MY WOUNDS HEALING ALL MY PAINS AND SORROWS.
>
> -PSALM 147:3

After sharing this lesson with the congregation on that Sunday, many were blessed and felt a need to ask God to give them a clean heart. This also showed me that I still had heart issues that need to be dealt with. I stayed on the path of asking God to fix my brokenness, to change me and give me a clean heart. I began to pray for a release of joy, peace, and happiness in my life.

God was calling me and I was not listening.

Lily (The Saving Grace)

There is no fear in love; but perfect love casteth out fear: because fear hath torment. He that feareth is not made perfect in love.

-1 John 4:18

I sat in silence as they both said, "Mom you won't have to do anything at all. We will feed her, take her out, play with her and we will keep everything clean and neat. We promise we will take care of her ourselves and you won't have to do anything," said my daughter, over and over, speaking for both her and my son. At that point, I already knew they would say anything to make me say yes to a pet. I had never been exposed to animals as a child and my mom always reiterated to us that animals were dirty and did not belong inside the home; I didn't even like stuffed animals. I kept weighing out the pros and cons and that if I got them a dog, I would not be able to touch it because their bodies felt weird to me. I knew that if I allowed the children to have a pet, especially inside, my family would never come over to visit us again.

I was very unsure, as the door opened and six tiny puppies came bouncing into the room. The door was quickly closed behind them to ensure they did not escape. Two of them were nervous and pooped on the floor immediately. I looked from a distance but did not touch. That was another one of my issues, I knew I would not be able to deal with any urine and poop inside. The children instantly began to pick up the puppies and play with them. Little Calvin's favorite was a boy, but someone else wanted that one. So all three of us came together and decided on a girl with a beautiful grayish brindle coat. Collectively we decided her name would be Lily Grace Breeze. She was very nervous and kept crawling up behind Little Calvin trying to hide. We began to pick up little things we needed to care for her and we picked her up a week later in a box wearing a diaper. As far as maintaining a puppy, I had no idea where to start. Went away for the weekend and came home to find that Calvin Sr., Maya and Little Calvin had already trained her to use it outside. I was delighted.

I felt that the children had been forced to deal with the shift in the home with the divorce, the least I could do was get them something they really wanted which was a dog. I was also thinking that this would help with teaching them to be more responsible. A schedule was devised in order to help the two of them work together to take care of Lily. The fact of the matter is that Lily may have really been for me from the beginning as God used Lily to teach me many things about myself. For the first couple of weeks, it was like having a new born baby in the house for the first time. She whined, ate, slept and pooped. I did not touch her at all; although, I thought she was absolutely adorable. I was working through my phobia at my own pace. Finally after she had followed me around back and forth for a month, without me touching her, one day I just reached down and rubbed her. I felt a sense of pride and freedom. She was so excited she started wagging her tail and tried to jump up in my arms. This milestone did not change the fact that I was still somewhat miserable because she was doing what she came to do, which was show me some things about myself. She made me realize that my control issues were bigger than I thought. A dog is going to be a dog, but I wanted her to do exactly what I wanted her to do, when I asked her to do it. One of my friends, Joshua, is great with dogs and agreed to help me train her. We had a training session at the park one day and it was Lily's first time being at the park. I wanted her to sit still beside me but her curiosity would not allow her to sit still. She insisted on playing in the dirt and moving around to take in her surroundings and watch the other dogs. I was quickly reminded that she was a dog and that is what they do. I realized that my fear and dislike for dogs had been instilled in me as a child. Really, I loved them and found that they just want to please their owners and be loved much like humans. During the training process, I learned that I had to love Lily where she was, just like God loves us. She showed me unconditional love!

> TO FIND
> SOMETHING YOU
> CAN ENJOY IS FAR
> BETTER THAN
> FINDING
> SOMETHING YOU
> CAN POSSESS.
>
> -GLEN HOLM

Lily became the nucleus of the family and she was what everyone needed for the season. She was known as the Saving Grace. She became Little Calvin's best friend. They played so hard together as if they were both boys. He would look forward to getting home from school each day to play with her. Lily found it very difficult to wait for him to finish his homework after school as she was ready to play as soon as he entered the door. Maya, being a nurturer would treat Lily like her baby. She would pick Lily up and cradle her in her arms and Lily would love that as she snuggled close. It was so funny that Lily would not allow anyone else to hold her that way.

To the Edge

Lily quickly became MY dog. I took her out every morning before I left for work, then I took her out to run and play in the evenings after work and worried about her always. The more I did, the less the children did. They loved Lily, but they were still children and they did not understand the idea of taking care of something every day, no matter how you feel and no matter what else you have to do. It took more than Little Calvin playing with her and Maya coddling her. The fact that I had grown to love her did not change the fact that I was broken and I resented those things that I should have appreciated. She greeted me each day after a long day at work by jumping on me and showing me love. She loved to lick my toes and sit on my feet and of course this frustrated me. She followed me continuously and when I went into my bedroom (where she was not allowed) she would sit at the door and whine for me until I came out.

One day as I vented to Joshua about Lily and how I may have to give her away. He reminded how good Lily was doing with training and gave me his famous line which was, "It is a process, be patient." He then calmly and casually asked me what else I had gotten rid of because it was not just the way I wanted it to be? He quickly expressed that I did not need to answer him but it was asked in order to evoke thought. That Joshua, he succeeded again, because this question caused me to think intensely and realize even more about myself. I was guilty of setting my own expectations for others and then being frustrated with them when they did not meet them. Finally, once Lily's job was complete, I did have to release her. I gave her up for adoption. The children were really not happy about this, but then neither was I. It was much harder than I thought it would be. Many tears were shed and many days and nights were spent missing her. Little Calvin felt that he had lost his best friend and Maya felt she had lost her baby.

> SOME
> RELATIONSHIPS
> CHANGE AND
> SOME SHOULD
> COMPLETELY END
>
> -LProctorM

Lily had shown me that it was ok to truly open up and love others believing that all they wanted from me was love in return (no ulterior motive), that I had control issues, that I love dogs, that my brokenness was causing me to be frustrated with those things that I should appreciate and she encouraged me to change that. God also used Lily to help me with my patience. The greatest lesson of all that I learned from Lily was unconditional love. She showed me unconditional love, the kind that only God gives. When I scolded her, she came right back to me and let me rub her belly. When I told her to move she continued to come back and when I showed frustration because she was lying at my door whining when I was in my room, she continued to show me love. Even my own children show me that they are not happy with me when I chastise them. Lily's actions made me stop and think about the unconditional love that God shows all of us. We as people don't always follow his commandments and we do things that he doesn't like, yet he continues to love us and show us patience, grace and mercy. I am so grateful that he does not throw us away when we sin, fail to follow his commandments and don't act like he wants us to act. We would all be in trouble if God acted like us. God loves genuinely and forgives easily. After my experiences with Lily, I was able to open my heart more freely to others that I would not have opened up to before. Lily was instrumental in helping me during my transformation. I was clearly out of my comfort zone. Having a dog, touching a dog, loving a dog, and caring for a dog was really a milestone for me. I will always appreciate that time and Lily will forever be a special memory and a part of my heart.

God was calling me and I was not listening.

Pick Up the Pieces

"Hope deferred maketh the heart sick, but when the desire cometh, it is a tree of life"

-Proverbs 13:12

While in Greenville, visiting my family, I went to Church with them one Sunday. As the service began, I knew that I was not there by chance because I now look for God in every situation. I had gone with the expectation of hearing from God. The pastor took his text from Proverbs 13:12, "Hope deferred maketh the heart sick, but when the desire cometh, it is a tree of life." And his subject was "Pick up the Pieces"

When he said the words pick up the pieces, I began to think about how I realized I was broken and how when I realized it, I asked God to fix me. But did I take the time to pick up all the pieces and take them to God? When you break something of importance and want to get it repaired, you must gather all of the pieces in order to have it repaired. I had been hurt, discouraged, frustrated, tossed and turned through many of life's situations and some of my pieces were scattered, some lost, some tucked away and some I tried to hide. It was time to muster up the strength and courage to gather all the pieces. All the pieces consisted of different colors and emotions, my tears, fears, joys, my will, my creativity, my ups and downs, my successes and my failures; all the pieces that collectively make me who I am. Once all of the pieces are given to God, he can then use what he wants to put me back together. It may be that some of the pieces will be scrapped. I may have been carrying some pieces of dead weight and God was now going to rid me of them. Only he knows how to salvage us and make us perfectly whole. He created us fearfully and wonderfully but as we go through life, we pick up unnecessary things and allow impurities to attach themselves to us, and we take on a lot of extra baggage and we don't know how to get rid of it.

Once the pieces are all put back together, I must go through the process of learning who I am all over again. God created me so he has the template. Who better to help you learn yourself than the one who created you? He knows what he put in me and what he is expecting out of me. Again, all things go directly back to God. Who better to ask to repair a broken product than the manufacturer?

I was reminded of when my children were very young, they depended on me to fix everything. My son loved transformers and he liked to take things apart and if he could not get them back together, he would collect all of the pieces and bring them to me or daddy to fix. He would be so frustrated about not being able to put all the pieces together but he would stand and watch intensely as we worked with it. That's how we should all be with God our father. The Pastor said that someone's breakthrough is in the anointing that is in my broken pieces. When the children were small, we also put puzzles together often. I always told them that it was very important that they did not lose any of the pieces of the puzzle because if so, the puzzle could not be put together completely, thus causing us to not get the full picture that was intended when the puzzle was created. Every piece is vitally important to the picture. That gave me another perspective of my brokenness and I realized that God had to break me in order to make me. No time to waste, I have been broken long enough. I must gather all the pieces to ensure that nothing is missed and not complain about this process but I must make haste. In my studies, I was reminded of how the Israelites stayed wandering in the wilderness for 40 years and the trip should only have taken eleven days. The moment the Israelites set out for the "Promised Land" they began to complain about their hardships, the food (lack of meat) among other things. Their complaining angered God. They were disobedient and showed no faith in God and therefore they were not allowed to enter the Promised Land. Like the Israelites in the wilderness, Christians are between promise and fulfillment. How are you handling the wilderness? Are you just wandering in the wilderness or are you trusting and obeying God? The Israelites turned back when the road ahead looked difficult. They did not want to be out of their comfort zone. They failed to obey God's instructions and trust in his promises. Is there something in your life that you know God wants you to do, but you have not because of fear, or lack of faith. Humble yourself before the Lord, seek his help,

> THE MORE IMPORTANT SOMETHING IS TO THE HEART, THE MORE RESISTANCE YOUR BODY FEELS.
>
> -STEVEN PRESSFIELD

and "make every effort to enter that rest."

I also thought of how T.D Jakes once said that we are drowning in what we are supposed to be walking on. God may have needed me to be broken in order to do a work in me, but I have made the process take longer than necessary. I was drowning in the pain of being broken instead of allowing God to mend me and use me. Yes there is a process for everything, but we make the process take longer than necessary when we resist what God is doing, or when we doubt him or start to complain about our situation rather than thank him and go along with him. I have been broken long enough! Where is the happy me, the fulfilled me, the joyful me, the peaceful me, the anointed me? I must forgive every hurt and pain, pick up the pieces and allow God to finish the work that he has begun in me. For of this I am confident, that He who has begun a good work in you will complete it until the day of Christ Jesus. (Philippians 1:6)

When God is working on you, it does not feel good. The pain of growth is not easy to handle. There were many days that I wanted so badly to go back to what was comfortable. God had already made it where I no longer had that as an option. Some days I would just burst into tears and tell God thank you for loving me too much to leave me broken the way that I was. I can remember the time that I took my son to the doctor because he was complaining of pain in his legs when walking. His doctor just laughed and said that he was experiencing growing pains and that the pain was normal. I can remember as a little girl going through puberty, there was pain that came along with lying on my stomach because of my growing chest. Then as a pregnant woman, the bigger the baby got the more pain and discomfort I felt because the baby was growing inside of me. So it is in the natural, so it is in the spirit.

Growth and pain go hand in hand. We have to trust that God will not put any more on us than we can bear. I was being challenged in every area of my life and on every side to grow. A certain amount of fear and uncertainty go along with growth as well. Along with the growth, God is requiring me to make some movement.

God was calling me and I was not listening

The Balancing Act...Starting With the One Within

Snuggle in God's arms when you are hurting, when you feel lonely, left out-let him cradle you, comfort you, reassure you of his all – sufficient power and love.

-Kay Arthur

I had hidden and masked pain and hurt for so long that it had become a part of me like a comforting security blanket that went along with me everywhere I went. Hiding the pain only prolongs the hurt. I thought I had forgiven and let go of the hurt but it was very much alive and I was harboring it. As a result, it was holding me hostage against my will and without my knowledge. It was tucked away like a needle in a haystack. I began to expect hurt and pain to come along with every situation. I would expect the worst, so that if it happened I was prepared, and then I would say, "I told you that would happen." Little did I know, this was causing me to become negative and go against my own beliefs. I would speak the positive but expect the negative. As a Christian, this is an awful place to be in because we know better and we should always trust God and know that what he said in his word will always prevail.

God wants us to be either hot or cold, but he is not pleased with us being luke warm. All things will work for the good of those who love the Lord (Romans 8:28. I would cover up the pain with a pleasant face and no one ever knew because I never let anyone really get close enough to know the difference. I learned to cope with the pain by helping others. My misery made me work harder to make others happy. I was truly an exception to the saying that, "Misery loves Company". I was the opposite, going out of my way, day after day, to make sure that no one had to suffer silently as I did, became normal for me. When I felt the absolute worst, I would repeat Isaiah 58:8 which says, "My light shall break forth like the morning and my healing (my restoration and the power of a new life) shall spring forth speedily." I was really expecting my new life to spring forth.

> GOD DOES NOT COMFORT US TO MAKE US COMFORTABLE, BUT TO MAKE US COMFORTERS.
>
> -JOHN HENRY JOWE II

For the most part, I had gone through a broken marriage and a divorce alone.

There were so many times that I felt that I wanted from my father. The fact of the matter was that although my parents were married for over 30 years before he died and we lived right in the same house together, my father and I did not have a relationship and I did not really know him. I could only go to God as my father and I always wanted him to just hold me, lock me in and let me snuggle with him. It is only God that can truly make us feel safe. Oh how I long to crawl up on his lap and hide those times that I was hurting the most. I would share only bits and pieces with a carefully selected two people, after suffering silently for so long. At that point, I vowed to be there for any and all hurting women whenever possible. I did not want anyone to suffer silently as I did. I always knew that prayer worked but I did not always know exactly what to pray for so I spent a lot of time saying, "Lord, help me, fix me and change me." I would always finish the prayer with "Thank you, Lord". Finally God said, "Enough". It was time to free the captive that had been held inside. Only God could find a needle in a haystack and pull it out. I needed his deliverance and I needed him to heal the broken one within and fast. This is why it is so important to continue to pray and trust God. Even when you don't know exactly what you need or quite how to ask him for what you do need, always pray and give thanks. He knows what we have need of and is faithful in giving it to us.

To the Edge

I began to have what I called "Chat n Chew" meetings at my home. I invited several young ladies over and it was intended to be a safe haven for us to come together and be lifted up. We came together to eat, talk, pray, laugh, comfort and be comforted. At the beginning of the meetings we gave praise reports and at the end we gave prayer requests. This was an opportunity for me to pray for someone other than myself and to focus on encouraging others to grow. Out of the Chat n Chews, friendships were developed, spiritual gifts were birthed, hearts were strengthened and prayers were answered. Just to think, this was birthed out of my pain. This forced me to give out of my own pain and although I did share part of my testimony with the ladies, no one meeting was used to discuss my pain, scars or hurt, but rather used to help and be there for the ladies. The ladies are all special to me and they helped me more than they will ever know.

After years of hurt and brokenness, my divorce and coming to the realization that I was broken, I began to pick up the pieces and ask God to heal the broken one within. I was hurting so bad, but I would repeat daily Psalm 147:3, "He heals my broken heart and binds up my wounds (curing my pains and sorrows). He began to work on me, which felt as though he was breaking me even more. The healing process itself is painful. Every day I felt like I was been crushed a little more. So many times I wanted to say please stop the pain but I have a friend that always says that if you stop the pain, you also stop the healing. I began the healing process of by getting to know myself.

I realized that I am a great person with a lot to offer. I had always catered to those that I cared about, not out of weakness, but out of the desire to see them happy because I wasn't. If anyone was going to be inconvenienced, it was going to be me. This made me hurt myself trying not to hurt them. I finally realized that this was not pleasing to God because I was wonderfully and fearfully made by him. I praise you because I am fearfully and wonderfully made; your works are wonderful, I know that full well. (Psalm 139:14)

God loves each of his children so much and wants us all to have peace and joy and prosper and be in good health.

For my family, I would buy their favorite foods, cook their favorite meals and do other things to make them comfortable. They appreciated me but I don't know if they knew to what extent I was sacrificing myself for them. My husband had always encouraged me to do what I liked or hang out with my friends. I was the one who chose to stay home and take care of them. In my quest to learn me, I made many trips to many places that may seem unimportant to some. One day, I went to get ice cream and tried all of the ice cream flavors to see which flavor I liked. I knew what kind Calvin Sr. liked, and the kids liked so that is the kind I bought from the store. What I didn't know, until that day, was what kind Regina liked. Another day, I went to rent a movie. I had always defaulted to horror, action or science fiction because that was what they liked. I elected not to choose any of those, instead I chose drama and comedy. Pizza, being my favorite food, was even compromised. Whenever ordering pizza for the family, I had always ordered one meat lover's thin and crispy (Calvin Sr.'s favorite) and one pepperoni hand tossed (the kids' favorite). After consideration, I realized, I prefer supreme pan pizza. This journey has been interesting and it has shown me why both knowing yourself and having balance in your life is so important. It is also important to remember to enjoy the journey.

When I think of balance, I think of balancing my checkbook, making sure my credits are labeled clearly so that my balance will reflect exactly the amount that I have available in the account. I also think of exercise when I think of balance. My balance is not the greatest in the gym. My challenge is strengthening my core so that my balance is better. Whenever I use the exercise ball, I must focus because it takes my body and my mind working together in order to stay on the ball. Webster's definitions of balance is a state of equilibrium or equipoise, equal distribution of weight, amount, etc.; a state of bodily equilibrium or mental steadiness or emotional stability; habit of calm behavior, judgment; etc. In life, we must learn to balance. It makes no difference how strong we are; if there is no balance, there is an issue.

As women, we must learn to balance being a loving and supportive wife without losing our own identities. We must learn to be great mothers and take good care of our children without neglecting ourselves. Must balance being a good Christian and live in this world without keeping our heads in the clouds Always heard the older and wiser say that we cannot afford to be so heavenly minded that we are no earthly good. We must continue to work out and exercise our bodies, feed our minds, stay sexy, work hard, play hard, love hard and pray even harder for ourselves and our families. If we don't feel good about ourselves and keep ourselves together, our families will end up being the ones to suffer. We must remember that we were women before we became wives and mothers and we still have our wants, needs, likes and dislikes.

God was calling me and I was not listening.

Dangling Arms

One of the greatest discoveries a man makes, one of his great surprises, is to find he can do what he was afraid he couldn't do.

-Henry Ford

On June 7, 2013 I was called to the President's office at the University where I had worked for the past eight years. I knew what this meeting was all about and all I wanted was to get it over with. God had already prepared me for what was to come. The night before, while talking to a friend, I said, "I don't have a good feeling about tomorrow. I feel like something is going to happen." I tried to play it off because I did not want to get him alarmed as well, but I really had a feeling that there would be trouble at work. At least 20 people were laid off including my whole department. There were several things that made me confident that it was in God's plan for me to be laid off. I was almost in awe about the sense of peace that I had after hearing the President say that my position had been eliminated. There was no panic, no fear and no tears, only peace. This had been coming for quite some time.

My mind went back to May 19th when I was at Church. Pastor William Murphy said that some of us need to stop wasting time and do what God has called us to do. He had us to repeat "I will not waste another 3 years doing something that has nothing to do with what God has anointed me to do. I will seek him diligently and allow him to move me into my purpose." We started a 21 day fast to run from May 22 – June 11th. I never would have expected this to happen the last week of the fast. I realize that purpose was pushing me from where I was, to where I was destined to be. God was removing every distraction from my life. No more excuses. I had asked God for more time for years. "What will I do with it now that I have it", I thought.

I never liked being vulnerable as this made me feel weak. I felt that if I avoided being vulnerable, I could avoid being hurt. This was not true. It takes a great deal of strength to be vulnerable.

> TO EARN THE
> RIGHT FOR
> OTHERS TO
> EXPRESS THEIR
> VULNERABILITIES,
> I TOO MUST
> BECOME
> VULNERABLE.
>
> -LProctorM

To the Edge

Again, God was trying to get me out of my comfort zone. I liked to play it safe. No matter how much I had always heard and understood that if you keep doing the same thing over and over you will keep getting the same results, I was too afraid to change what I was doing. It was time for me to step out and have enough faith to do something different and allow what was in me to come out. As humans, most of us do nothing when we are afraid. It is easier to sit in the seat of mediocrity than it is to say goodbye to fear and move forward to greater. Fear is designed to hold us back and keep us afraid of the circumstance and afraid of the solution.

There is a quote by Guillaume Apollinaire that reads,

"Come to the edge,' 'We can't. We're afraid.' 'Come to the edge.' 'We can't. We will fall!"Come to the edge.' And they came. And he pushed them. And they flew."

I had read this quote as a young girl and was drawn to it. I made a copy of it and kept it in my treasure box and would read it every now and then.

> "COME TO THE EDGE, 'WE CAN'T. WE'RE AFRAID.' 'COME TO THE EDGE. 'WE CAN'T. WE WILL FALL!' 'COME TO THE EDGE.' AND THEY CAME. AND HE PUSHED THEM. AND THEY FLEW."
>
> -GUILLAUME APOLLINAIRE

Not knowing that it was literally for me. God has been calling me to the edge for years but I was not listening. Little did I know that healing for my brokenness was at the edge; and that joy, peace, and my breakthrough was at the edge.

I chose to walk all that time causing my journey to take that much longer when God had given me the ability to fly. God needed me to relax my arms so that while they were dangling, he could release the wind under them like wings in order for me to fly. Fear had held me back. Finally, I understood "God has not given me the spirit of fear but of power, and of love, and of a sound mind." II Timothy 1:7

It is time to allow God to be God in my life. I am learning to allow my arms to just dangle at my sides signifying that God has control and not me. Whenever I start to feel tense or worry about something, I will say, "Dangling arms, Regina!" People that study body language say that when you cross your arms, you are being defensive or trying to keep others out and maintain control. I can remember how I had always held my arms, tightly folding them both across my chest when talking to people. If I was sitting down, I also crossed my legs. As I became a little more comfortable, I would relax one arm holding my hand under my chin until finally relaxing both arms signifying my letting people in slowly. This was all done subconsciously. There was a time during the transition of unfolding my arms that I had to learn to sit on my hands until I could allow them to dangle at my side. I have decided that dropping my arms totally means that I am surrendering to God, showing him that I realize that I have no control, nor do I want to control what he is responsible for. I have always been the type to want to be in control. Well he has put me in a position to show me that I really don't have the control that I thought I had. I surrender all to God. As I take this

Regina Breeze

long tough walk to the edge, my arms are dangling at my side showing that I am humbly following God.

I had to give myself permission to just be. Apostle Wyett always says, "I be what God says I be, I be it now, and I be nothing less!"

Love Is...

"Love is patient, love is kind. It does not envy, it does not boast, it is not proud, it does not dishonor others, it is not self-seeking, it is not easily angered, it keeps no record of wrongs. Love does not delight in evil but rejoices with the truth. It always protects, always trusts, always hopes, always perseveres ."

-1 Corinthians 13: 4 - 8

During my alone time, God began to deal with me on Love. The concept of love was presented to me on three different occasions within a week. I knew that it was time for me to check my heart and deal with my perception or concept of love. This process of love had already begun with Lily and her lesson for me on unconditional love. God says in Deuteronomy 6:5, "And thou shalt love thy God with all thine heart, and with all thy soul, and with all thy might." God also instructed us to love thy neighbor as thyself. Those are huge requests but in order to please God, we must honor them. The question that kept coming to my mind was "Does anyone actually love the way that God commanded us to love?"

One Sunday, while in Church the pastor's message was "Moving into Supernatural Love" and it was powerful. She broke down the three types of Greek love which are Eros, Phileo and Agape. Upon listening and following up with my own studying I found that we all operate on different levels of love with different people and at different times without giving any real thought to it. Eros deals with the body. The word comes from erotic and is used to express sexual love between two people. An expression of feelings of arousal intended for marriage, this love has been misused. Phileo deals with the soul and is the love of wisdom. This love is the brotherly love that is part of the emotions and warm affection shown to family and friends. Agape love comes from the spirit. This is a self-sacrificing love that keeps record of no wrong. Do you love God unconditionally?

Do you love others unconditionally or even genuinely; your spouse, your children, your friends? Love is not about expecting someone to do just what you want them to do and be just what you want them to be. Unconditional love is allowing people to do what they do, accepting them for who they are, and not judging them, but loving them genuinely anyway.

I then began to listen to the Love Letter series by T.D. Jakes and I found that I, like most people, had not mastered love. We use the word too loosely. God loved us so much that he sacrificed his only son on the cross for our sins. This was the ultimate sacrifice. What greater love than a man who would lay down his own life for another? Abraham showed his love to God through his obedience when he was told to go to the mountain and offer his son as a sacrifice to God. Because of Abraham's obedience, God had a ram in the bush and he did not have to sacrifice his son. The fact that Abraham took his son and headed to the mountain and prepared his son for sacrifice showed his obedience and his love for God. Sometimes God just wants to see if we will love and trust him enough to obey him. How many of us would sacrifice our children for anything or anybody? How many of us would sacrifice our own life for another? We can't just love who we feel like and when we feel like it. We cannot stop loving people because they do us wrong and we cannot just love those people who are most like us, who share our race, our religion, our economic status, who work with us, or who live with us. I must love my children enough to allow them to make their own mistakes in life and grow. I had to love my husband enough to let him go even though I wanted us to work it out.

People have many interpretations of love. Some mistake sex and lust for love. Others try to buy love, while some look for love in the wrong places. While others avoid love like the plague because they are afraid of being hurt, they don't want to appear vulnerable or they just don't want to make the sacrifice.

Regina Breeze

Webster's definitions of the word love are as follows

noun

1. a profoundly tender, passionate affection for another person.

2. a feeling of warm personal attachment or deep affection, as for a parent, child, or friend.

3. sexual passion or desire.

verb *(used with object)*

1. to have love or affection for: All her pupils love her.

2. to have a profoundly tender, passionate affection for (another person).

I surveyed a few people to find out their interpretation of love. I have captured a few of the responses below.

1. Love is a powerful emotion that is shared between people that are important to each other. **(Maya) – 14**

2. Love is the reason that we are here. Without love God would not have made us and he would not have been so tolerant with us over the years that we have made so many mistakes. **(Calvin, Jr.) – 11**

To the Edge

3. Love knows no boundaries. It is crazy and it does not judge.

4. Love is a word of obligation. It means commitment and is a conscious decision to commit. True love will always operate in spite of...

5. I am in love with love and being in love! Not for one particular person or thing, but love itself. I do desire to have a loving and meaningful relationship. I love what love is, how it feels, how it makes others feel and the motivation that comes from it for life, people, days, nights, work, resolution, giving, taking, learning and so much more that would take me days to list.

6. Unloved feels all of the same but opposite. We seek behaviors that make us feel loved. Sadly, they only supply us temporarily. In the place of not having it, feeling it, and knowing it; we eat, shop, spend, drink, work and abuse...whatever we need to feel better in the place of love. God made us in love and this is why we cannot

74

do without it. I wish I could create a love pill, write everyone a prescription so that it could be picked up at any time without a co-pay.

7. God, I love you for loving me! Now I need to learn to depend on that love.

8. Love is unconditional, no if ands or buts, the same way Jesus Christ loves us.

9. Love means having endurance and strength. Being whole and complete.

10. Love is wholeness, blind and forgiving. Love is being selfless and naked. It is the ultimate sacrifice, the greatest gift and the greatest sense of freedom. God is love and love is God.

11. Love is a feeling of emotion for someone. It can be altered or changed due to situations or circumstances. It does not have to be earned (like with your children) but can be developed over time.

12. Love covers a multitude of faults

On the heels of the survey, I decided to have a chat n chew with a few girlfriends. We came together to discuss love. First sharing the results of the survey, we found the different interpretations of love to be interesting. The definitions were different depending on the gender. Some spoke of love in the emotional sense and others spoke of love in the spiritual sense. After discussing what love means to each of us and how it has affected us, we shared personal experiences and gleaned more on the subject.

We then did a powerful exercise with 1 Corinthians 13:4-7.

"Love is patient, love is kind. It does not envy, it does not boast, it is not proud, it does not dishonor others, it is not self-seeking, it is not easily angered, it keeps no record of wrongs. Love does not delight in evil but rejoices with the truth. It always protects, always trusts, always hopes, always perseveres."

In these scriptures, love is broken down and expressed quite clearly. We went line by line having each person share where she is, what she is doing well and what she still needs to work on. This was a great exercise, showing that we could all do better in one area or another. Talking it out also helped us see our weaknesses and get wisdom from others regarding them. God demands that we love him as well as each other; and although it is a great request, he would not have commanded it if it were not possible. It was interesting for me to see how far I have come since God began transforming me. For example, love is patient. I have always struggled in the area of patience and now I can actually say that I have gotten a lot better and will continue to get better in this area. I saw the difference in some of the other areas as well and I also know where I need the work. It takes putting forth some thought and effort and we must make it a priority to love on purpose.

There is so much to be said about love that no one conversation, chat n chew, seminar, meeting or event is enough time to discuss it and cover all of the bases and do the subject justice. God says in 1 Corinthians 13:1 – 3, "Though I speak with the tongues of men and of angels, and have not love: I am become as sounding brass, or a tinkling cymbal. And although I have the gift of prophecy, and understand all mysteries and all knowledge; and though I have all faith, so that I could remove mountains, and have not love, I am nothing." This further reiterates how important love is and that without it we are nothing and we have nothing.

To the Edge

Love is like a beautiful rose and we pulled it apart a petal at a time to get to the root of what God wanted us to walk away with. Love never fails and we may give up on it, but love never gives up on us. True love originated with God and without him, we cannot love as we should. Quite simply GOD IS LOVE!

I proceeded to ask God to teach me how to love him as well as others the way he commanded. I once heard someone say that the root of all sin is selfishness, so I then questioned whether I had been holding back and being selfish. I believe this is why God has been presenting love to me repeatedly and I am being tested in the area of love and I must pass this test. He needed me to evaluate myself and understand that it is not just about me. During this test, I must evaluate how I treat my friends and family and especially how I interact with my own children, whom I love so dearly. For fear of being hurt, I found it hard to love those that were closest to me freely. Those people, I loved carefully and defensively, always keeping a part of me on reserve. I asked God to heal me in every broken area, give me a pure heart and make me a loving woman. Love is innocent and has no motives or hidden objectives. Therefore I should only expect to be loved genuinely and to love the same. My desire is to love purely, genuinely, and unselfishly. Honestly, I needed God to not only teach me to love but how to receive love as well. Going along with my transformation, although I have never wanted to, God is calling me to love outside of my comfort zone, to "Love on the Edge."

> LOVE RECOGNIZES NO
> BARRIERS. IT JUMPS
> HURDLES, LEAPS FENCES,
> PENETRATES WALLS TO
> ARRIVE AT ITS
> DESTINATION OF HOPE.
>
> **-MAYA ANGELOU**

It was not enough to discuss love at the chat n chew and read those surveys; I felt that there was more for me to do. I decided to take on my own love challenge, starting with studying all of the scriptures on love. I began to look for ways to show love to others. Not just showing love, but saying, "I love you". Deciding to give others their flowers while they are alive, I came up with ways to tell them how I feel about them constantly. Expressing love and appreciation goes a long way.

To the Edge

God was calling me and I was beginning to listen

Time of Solitude

"Many people suffer from the fear of finding oneself alone, and so they don't find themselves at all."
— Rollo May

I have never had so much free time, alone time, quiet time in my whole life. It feels as if God has placed a wall around me and I have been stripped of many outside influences. Not only was God calling me closer to him, but he was calling me to get to know myself in him as well. I had gone through the period where I reconnected with Regina, my likes and my dislikes and now I needed to reconnect with who I am in God. Develop that personal relationship with God and do my first works again. Here I am spending quality time with God and with myself. How often do we actually have the opportunity to get to know ourselves? Do we like the person that we are? Often we use noise, others and outside stimulus to keep from dealing with ourselves.

Os Hillman speaks of an isolation chamber by saying that while in the chamber, God is calling us aside to fashion something new in us. The isolation chamber is designed to call us to deeper roots of prayer and faith. It is not a comfortable place and it is only for a season.

Needless to say, I had also never been so lonesome in my life. I have really had to stay focused on God because I could not have done any of this on my own. Since college, I have always been a busy bee, working on this or working on that, busy with this or busy with that, trying to figure out how to juggle this and that so that I could get everything that I needed to do done. Now, I believe that God has granted me a time of rest, recuperation, refining and preparation. He has removed all distractions so that he could work on me, speak to me and have me hear him clearly. Because of this I could do those things that I was created to do without excuses or hesitation. During this alone time, God pointed out some things to me about myself. It was in the alone time that I was really able to see what I am made of. I did not know my own strength. God put everything that I needed for this time in me when he created me. I feel that God has allowed me to feel lonely also to show me how to be careful and not judge others for mistakes that they make and to help me in the area of showing compassion. Realization hit me that I can really be hard on people sometimes when they make mistakes and none of us are perfect.

I had gone from working diligently in a church for over four years to not having an established membership with a church. God was showing me that the Church was in me and not in the

82

building. I needed to develop and nourish the church in me. There were times that I was physically at church and I was not focusing on God. I was singing on the praise team but not able to go deeper into worship due to distractions. I was listening to the Pastor's message but not able to focus because I was worried about the next thing. Did I make enough visitors' bags? Are there enough bulletins? Are there enough tithing envelopes? Are the children in place and behaving? Do we have enough food for the guests? If there was an evening class or program, was everything in place for that?

One day I read a post from a friend that said, "That we should all take time to Be Quiet and Be Still in order to hear his voice and allow God to work in our lives." When Jesus quieted the storm in Mark 4:39, he first said, "Quiet! Be still!" Then the wind died down and it was completely calm.

I felt that God was talking directly to me. I had entirely too much noise going on inside of me. At that time, the noise was not around me because I was alone most of the time. If you ask God and wait on him with expectation, he will show you things about yourself. He knew I needed the quiet time alone to silence myself, as my mind was always running and the enemy often used my own thoughts to hinder me. I am reminded of reading "Battlefield of the Mind" by Joyce Meyer. It is now that I am able to process some of the things I read. An idle mind is definitely the devil's workshop. This is why God says to meditate on him and his word daily. He also says that if we keep our mind on God, he will keep us in perfect peace. We must focus on Glory because we can't make it on our own. All of these words became more real to me during my period of solitude.

There were some days that I wondered if I was being tested to see if I would crack and go crazy or was this somehow building character and making me stronger? Clearly I was getting stronger while getting to know God and myself on a deeper spiritual level. My overwhelming desire to know more about him propelled me to seek him more in my alone time. Also I began to seek and expect encounters with God. Wanted to know more and more about him, for him to speak to me and tell me secrets. I made a conscious decision to choose peace. Instead of asking God for peace over and over, I began to choose it and pursue it and follow it. As I sought him, I encouraged others to seek him. During this period of solitude, the people I was normally around, I was no longer around. Some stopped calling me, and some I stopped calling. God was shaking things up in my life and stretching me beyond recognition. The few people that were around during the period of solitude were being used strategically by God in my life for a purpose. I'm not even sure if they knew that they were being used by God.

There were some times during my alone time that I felt as though I was going to burst or jump out of my skin. Anxiety, frustration, helplessness and excitement came on me all at the same time. I knew I was pregnant with purpose, but I also knew that I had no control of what God may ask of me. I would ask God over and over, "Am I using this time wisely, and are you pleased with me?"

There were also days that I felt the urge to take off running, away from myself (with no place to go). Every place I go, I was sure to be there. God was forcing me to deal with myself and with him. I was learning to know the good, the bad, the pretty and the ugly about me and was allowing God to change whatever needed to be changed.

God was calling me and I was listening.

Truth of Soles

You wonder how many days, solitude can I take. You thought it was a dark moment, hurricane that dim the earth.

Lost in a sea of emotions tempered with abstract pause. Painting a sky has never been so gray. Time; night and day no difference.

Love has never been so lonely, the sun never so cold. I'm lost with a map in a familiar land. Do I hold me, let go, move to the other end of the earth to find my truth. Trying to find my soul yet my soul is trying to find me.

How is it that we can't meet, they say it's great to know thyself; freedom is the key.

Never did I imagine freedom is not what it seems to be until free found me.

I'm a mess in perfect proportions yet still "Scream" on the wall celebrated for all the colors that I have. I may not be hard as a rock but still oil flows and sticks around.

My moment of darkness is a glimpse of my light that's unfamiliar to me. Caring about what I have is irrelevant when I can ponder what I had. It's all mine and I didn't know it but I get a peek and now sadden it me! Thanks for opening my shell, even though I'm dirty I'm still that butterfly flying in hell.

Do as you please; I'm an empty cup, use me.

-Joshua Arnold

The Awakening

The awakening deals with perception. My perception of my life and purpose was changed. God releases us according to his purpose and not ours. When I surrendered to his will and allowed my arms to dangle and got in the position to fly, something was awakened in me. After realizing that I was broken and that my family was under the pressure of trying to be the glue that held me together, I had a real conversation with God about my life. Today I feel better, I think better, I act better and I look better. I have been working hard trusting God to transform me spiritually, physically and emotionally. I am still a work in progress but as I stated before, I am so happy that God loved me too much to leave me the way I was.

> I AM HAPPIER. I GUESS I MADE UP MY MIND TO BE THAT WAY.
>
> -RALPH WALDO EMERSON

I thought about my journey and everything became clear. I had to share this journey. I always knew that I was supposed to write a book but it was not time because I was broken and I struggled with sharing and my arms were folded tightly. I was not allowing people in and I was not ready. God was calling me and I was not ready to hear him. When I finally began to hear him, I knew that I had no option but to write and share, as my full deliverance would come through the writing and sharing. I am reminded of one of my friends that passed four years ago. She would always tell me that I needed to stop playing and write the book because that's what's in me. This gives me meaning when I read the quote, "If you bring forth what is within you, what you bring forth will save you. If you do not bring forth what is within you, what you do not bring forth will destroy you." Gospel of Thomas

In a sense, writing this book is saving me. My deliverance comes with each chapter that is written and God is transforming me with the words that are written.

God took me through many stages to transform my life while putting me back together. I understand two things and they are that people do what is important to them and that people cannot change what they don't see.

Sometimes I ask myself, "If my family had stayed intact, how long would it have taken for me to realize that I was broken. I could never change my situation because I could not see it. I don't think it would have mattered if anyone had come out and said the words "You are broken" to me, until I saw it for myself, my situation may have never changed. I was broken and hurting badly, and as a result, I was hurting the people that I loved the most. I have always heard it said that hurt people hurt people and I was living proof of that. This is not something intentional, it is just a fact. One cannot do better until one knows better. When someone is hurting, everything is seen from the eyes of the pain. I have also always heard that we see things as we are and not as they are. We must learn to control our hurt and not allow our hurt to control us. Hurt and pain are a part of life and we cannot stop that but we can make it a priority to not allow it to consume us. Sometimes we try so hard to hold on to the very thing that God is trying to take from us. This is because we spend so much time worrying about what we think we are losing instead of what we are gaining. This also shows fear of the unknown and a lack of faith, when we try so hard to hold on and stay in our comfort zone.

For many years I held on tightly to the belief that God was going to restore my marriage. I had tunnel vision and I held on to that faith like no other. Believing so strongly and holding on so tightly that I was not putting any action to my faith. Holding on so tightly that even I could not breathe and was afraid to move for fear that the glue that was holding me together would begin to dissolve. I did not want anyone to try to help me for fear that all of the pieces of me would fall apart. As I began to let go, I began to realize that although I was holding tightly, things were already broken. I did not have enough faith to just let everything go and let all of the pieces fall and scatter and trust God to fix it. I thought I could control the pieces but I was broken and pieces of me were scattered but I was still trying to hold everything together and control all situations so as not to appear to be a failure. God wanted me to let go and really trust him. In all actuality this faith was paralyzing me. I was not letting go, nor was I putting any action to my faith. I was stuck in limbo and did not realize that I was holding even myself in a broken state and was not allowing myself to live. I should have let it go in the middle and trusted God to fix it rather than let it go at the end and then asking God why he did not fix it. God told me a long time ago to let it go and allow him to work.

When you are trusting and believing God for something, you must put action to your faith. You must trust that God knows how to do what needs to be done. It means that you have to remind yourself that God is almighty, omniscient and omnipresent.

He sits high and looks low. He is so big and certainly knows how to handle our small problems. God's time is not our time. He does not always do things just the way we think he should but he knows what we need. Don't allow your faith to be immobilized by your desires. You must consciously trust God and know that if he does not heal your body, he has a plan and it will still work for your good. If he does not fix your marriage, he has a plan and it will still work for your good. If he does not do exactly what we ask him to do, when we ask him to do it and the way we ask him to do it, he still has a plan and it will work for our good. This is what Faith coupled with trust is really about!

In my case, my faith was in releasing and letting go, and my lack of faith was shown in trying to hold on so tightly. It was not until I really let go that I found peace, joy and freedom. Once I let it go, I began to live. The glue that was holding me together had gotten weak and it was time to let it go as it was giving new meaning to crazy glue. I realized that at all cost, my biggest desire was to be whole and please God.

> THE VERY ACT OF
> BELIEVING
> CREATES
> STRENGTH OF ITS
> OWN.
>
> ANONYMOUS

If we love God, things will always work out for our good. I learned that Faith cancels out Fear. It takes faith to be vulnerable, to love unconditionally, to be successful rather than have a fear of failure, to be in a relationship and love someone without focusing on the possibility of being hurt. It takes faith to let your guard down and allow your arms to dangle, to awaken the giant, to walk to the edge and it certainly takes faith to share the story.

I am forced to live on Blind Faith. Although it is normal for me to feel that I should be doing something more, God is continuously telling me to "Be still and know that I am God" -Psalm 46:10.I am walking to the edge with God. The glue has been dissolved, all the pieces of me collected and put back together, and I have finally let go of all that I was holding on to.

To the Edge

Now that I am finally following God to the edge, would I want to go back? The answer is NO!

If I had to go back, I would Open my arms and hear, I would give love freely and allow myself to be loved, I would share myself and I would be unselfish. I would definitely take more time to enjoy the journey. In fact, I may still have wanted to walk for a good bit of time in order to enjoy the journey. This is a time for me to reflect on my present blessings and not dwell on my past misfortunes. I will still do all of these things while living on the edge.

For me the edge symbolizes confidence, strength, courage, freedom, wholeness and being at peace with myself and with God, knowing that I am not perfect but I am aware of who I am and who God has created me to be.

God has placed greatness in each of us. What's hiding in you? What strengths have God placed in you that are not being used? What gifts and talents are you allowing to lie dormant in you? I challenge you to get to know yourself. Seek God and find out what his plans are for your life. If you are broken, pick up the pieces and allow God to make you whole. If you are not broken, be thankful and allow him to do something else that needs to be done in your life.

Romans 8:28 says, "And we know that all things work together for good to them that love God, to them who are called according to his purpose." This story began where I thought my life was ending, and for the first time in my life, IT'S ALL COMING TOGETHER!!!

My prayer regarding healing, deliverance and wholeness:

Dear Heavenly Father,

I boldly come to your throne giving you thanks, glory honor and praise. I first ask that you forgive me for all of my sins and help me to walk upright before you. Thank you so much for allowing me to see that I was broken. Thank you most of all, for loving me too much to leave me in my broken state. I thank you for being patient with me while calling me to the edge for so long. Thank you for my husband and children and for sending me such wonderful friends, for they have all taught me so much.

Although it was painful, I thank you for the journey. Thanks for giving me the courage to pick up the pieces, for teaching me about love, for the time I had with Lily, for teaching me how to allow my arms to dangle, and for awakening the giant.

Thank you for not just calling me to the edge but for walking with me every step of the way. Thanks for comforting me so that I may comfort others and for entrusting me to help hurting women. Help me to continue to walk in the light and strive to be what you have called me to be. Please help me to remember and appreciate the journey while understanding that I am not perfect and I still have much to learn and miles to go before I sleep. Help me to grow beyond and never revert back to what was once my comfort zone.

Finally, I know that it was never about me at all. Thanks for giving me the strength and the courage to share and for allowing me to see that none of our experiences with you are just for us but to be used to help others. I give you all the glory. Amen!

Acknowledgements

-Special thanks to my mother and my siblings for all of your love, support and prayers. Mother thanks for instilling in me the importance and power of prayer. Without that foundation, I may not have been strong enough to make the journey. You all helped me more than you will ever know. I was never able to share this journey with you all because I had to walk it alone. God knew you all would have been my shield and crutch. That is why he moved me away from you in order to get me to the edge. Thank you and I love you very much.

Special thanks to Calvin, Sr., Maya and Calvin, Jr. for being a great family and for being the glue for as long as you were. Thanks for always encouraging me to be all that God created me to be. My sincere apologies for all the discomfort that I caused you as a result of my brokenness.

-Special thanks to Linda-Proctor Merritt for being a great friend. For taking the time to get to know me in spite of my folded arms and the wall around me and for not running away from me when I was broken.

-Special thanks to Joshua Arnold for being a great friend and for listening to me go on and on about the book, Lily, the gym and for not going along but giving me opposition when needed.

-Thanks to Johnny Brannon for always encouraging me and for pushing me to allow the giant to be awakened.

-Thanks to Jessie McFry and Telisa Vernon for being friends that encourage and for being as persistent as I was resistant to letting you in.

-Thanks to Somalia Brown for always listening and for having my back, praying with me and for me.

-Special thanks to Apostle Keith and Prophetess Shalita Wyett and Overseer Spencer Wright for giving me the unadulterated Word of God (being instrumental in my spiritual growth) and for encouraging me to keep writing the book even when I wanted to stop.

www.ingramcontent.com/pod-product-compliance
Lightning Source LLC
LaVergne TN
LVHW021402080426
835508LV00020B/2412